ORPHAN FIRE

ORPHAN FIRE

poems

ALISSA VALLES

Four Way Books
Tribeca

Editorial Office
Four Way Books
POB 535, Village Station
New York, NY 10014
www.fourwaybooks.com

Library of Congress Cataloging-in-Publication Data

Valles, Alissa.
Orphan fire : poems / Alissa Valles.
    p. cm.
"A Stahlecker series selection."
ISBN-13: 978-1-884800-87-0 (alk. paper)
ISBN-10: 1-884800-87-4 (alk. paper)
I. Title.
PS3622.A53O77 2008
811'.6--dc22
                        2008017237

This book is manufactured in the United States of America
and printed on acid-free paper.

Four Way Books is a not-for-profit literary press. We are grateful for the
assistance we receive from individual donors, public arts agencies,
and private foundations.

This publication is made possible with public funds from
the National Endowment for the Arts and from the
New York State Council on the Arts, a state agency.

Distributed by University Press of New England
One Court Street, Lebanon, NH 03766

[clmp]

We are a proud member of the Council of Literary Magazines and Presses.

This book is for Zdena

Contents

III

I

Why a little curtain of flesh on the bed of our desire?

—W. Blake

ORPHAN FIRE

i

Not a god's weapon of mass destruction, just a flint spark driven up a dry hillside,
on Ararat of course, let into the stables like a stray animal to share at the trough,
until an intruder stealing a horse saw it and thought he could make it work for him
down in the brothels of humanity; now anyone can touch it: junkies, canteen cooks
and poets, and for them it consumes its own origins, air, eagerness and brightness;
twice orphaned, by gods and by earth, just to give bodies of clay an hour's warmth

ii

Constant fire, passing into the created world
loses track of its source and destroys its end,

coming to know three kinds of life form: pain
of landscape, pain of language, pain of love.

A sea becomes a river, a cry becomes a word,
a "vivid thing in the air," the air around you.

iii   ב

so the closest you get to the first cause is this
thirst, the nearest you get to purity is the pain
of division, the hook of a nurse's arm pulling
you out, the hook of a harpoon pulling you in

3

iv

I lie in a glass box naked, turned to the light.
Taken out at intervals and fed someone else's
time: at top speed, from one socket to another.
The week ends with two candles held together.

From this beginning, there arises a question, or
a series of questions opening out of each other.
I hope to have the chance to speak about other,
more radiant forms of being in the near future.

But first a dream: flakes of cloud, descending,
catch fire when they touch the skin. It must be
matched by another heat from inside yourself.

Is it true there is a clock buried in each of us?
That love can take the form of telling the time
from somebody else's skin, but without hands?

v

You wanted a pure island language
blind to the world like a tree's root
but you drew a slip of paper saying:

a word like a hand that could reach
and touch the face of an angry child,
a dying man, and now you can't find

a word in any language that would
both bind a man to his own world
and lead him, trusting, into another.

There may be such a word, but how
to know to whose body it's attached,
from what world it is reaching out?

vi   **Atomic Love Poem**

The night sky with its cast of stars
shows the dailies for the production
free of charge to everyone involved

The warmth left in a seat on the bus
proves, against all odds, the raging
of some inextinguishable furnace

How even the dirtiest gutter rivulet
watched by a bum on the pavement
implies the wild liberties of oceans

Written on the inner slope of a teapot
in the color of brick and dried blood:
a secret tribal history of mankind

If this be so, why then from among
all the fantastic conflagrations
do I choose what claims to be you?

vii   **Body**

Map of water and shame,
ardent junk, congress
filled with the arguments of chemicals

Echo chamber for the cries
of stubborn generations, all the quaint invisibles
death has grown a beard on

Maze and flame,
factory where decay's people clock in,
philosopher-clown blowing a whistle at each epiphany

Washed by the rough nurse, morning,
wheeled into the wards of afternoons,
feeds exhausted on the broth of dusk

Reads the erratic cards of dreams
turns on insomnia's rack,
breaks into the safe of sleep

Loses its name in foreign embraces,
forges a passport to a country of tenderness,
gestures like a child at the thing that it wants,
opaque from its own breath on the glass

viii

There, where you turn left at a bridge
and follow a path's descent to water,
there, where pines are bitten by frost
in a valley unsheltered by mountains,
an oak holds winter in its black arms,
unmoving, yielding nothing to the eye
and grey angels are raking the needles;
there, where a river moves under the ice,
and the flash of a kingfisher is the only
measurement of time, and where breath
rushes forward like an animal staying
always just ahead of the hunter, it was
there I left from, a lighter in my pocket

& my body ran like Io down continents

ix

In the beginning the word *move*, a silent meal,
portraits of ancestors, code books and knives;

you descend the rusting river slowed by bends,
you sleep, a sparrow in the shape of its flight.

Gods' names lose their vowels, rituals harden;
drying like fossils, words sleep out in the cold.

When it comes time to move again, off you run
waving (slow motion) the long end of a curse.

Leave lightly as you arrived all those years ago.

x

Leaving a house on fire what did we take?
A suitcase full of smoke & untranslatable
jokes, words on ice, tongues torn from it,
confidential papers giving off a fragrance
of dry grass and salt, inflammable sheets,
a broken clock, a guidebook to the species,
the fur of a nocturnal animal, some names.

xi   **Esther**

Running by columns of lament, past dim gold and iron chains,
joy goes begging underground like an angel without a dowry,
and trips at the feet of a street preacher singing *desire shall fail.*

She, Esther, is justice's date, with a face already turned to fire;
here where the highway ends, and a dead fly is wiser than you –
leave your stilts here, go get lost, that is the way to your book.

xii

Later arrow that flew out from the soul

No hill, no house, nothing here to say *I*.
To see the world one obliterates oneself;
naked film bathing in the acid darkness.

In a field, an arrowhead still draws blood.
Death left its refuse, nests of human hair.
Which heaven? Sight's edge, light's husk.

xiii

In the same lowland landscape where your grandfathers
lost their last fistful of religion, you go looking for them.

Corn still summons the scythe, stones still court heights,
but the new sword, feather-light, falling, makes no sound.

Between an imperial coin and the gaping skull of a horse
ants drag a dragonfly's wing, a last illustration of Darwin.

Lyrical grasslands frame the greyish foreheads of cities
overgrown train tracks run alongside the shallow ditches

where before a passing eye the nettle-centurions bloom,
ratifying ceaselessly the pact of beauty with destruction.

xiv

Today I didn't bathe or dress or speak,
didn't read the paper or answer letters;
didn't work very much, maybe an hour
to placate the spiteful god Anonymous.

A house not mine was filled with light.
I walked the hallways talking to myself;
a butterfly, finding its way into a room,
beat its wings to shreds against the pane.

I would have told you if you'd been here.
You were saying that quattrocento angels
always seem surprised at nature's cruelty,
and this an advantage we had over them:

a cynical knowledge that helps us endure.
Today I wanted to ask – endure as what?
All day, cargo boats passed on the river;
gulls clipped the wide water like a ribbon.

Nothing surprises us; only beauty, a ribbon,
marks the distance between us and salvation.

xv

Sun pours from a pitcher of cloud,
a bus stands still at an intersection:

a woman kicks a crouching body
(dog or child), its howl runs out.

A fire held to the world's tongue.
Freedom begins to conceal itself.

We spoke other languages before
but they weren't necessarily better.

xvi

I lie under the winter, under a stone of cloud:
already the snow is being fitted to my throat
like the shirt an angel once laid out for Blake.

The mice are all my company; they occasion
doubt as to the sovereignty of my own mind,
the idea that man is a measure of everything.

The mice ate half a long white bread; now I'll
feed the rest to birds returning across the lake.

I can see the folds of a child's dress, imitating
wings in bold flight, without memory of a fall.

xvii   *Fear*

Against your spine it once hugged you
—you clung to it as if it were a brother,
it seemed to know something important

Quickly vain intelligence turned it to ice
and you wondered if it in fact might be
your heart and what fuel it could be fed,

how it could be melted down and yield
tears the right words or even a melody
before the glacier reached your throat

xviii

He brings his songs from another country
and even they are borrowed.

Dancing, he weeps.
Dancing, he grows angry.
The next journey will be brief.
Dancing, he laughs.

xix

So far it is my eyes, my judgment and my searching that speak these words to you

Water washing the lining of bodies and countries,
war games of whales, your pale nurse eucalyptus,

the science of goodbyes, laws of cities, irregular
verbs, a river circling a lake, a man selling leather

I'll tell you but first please tell me to what oracle
I pay tribute, who is speaking through me, whose

fire and invective, hands washing sheets, in whose
sky—a nest of light lasting no more than a second

hide and seek
in a cemetery

is all you know
a branch
brushing glass
a hand
touching a wall

xx   Draft for a Psalm

Night sky, voyaging stars, distant space: I can't hear what you're saying. A drunk
is singing in the yard, a cat chasing prey, a woman groping along a crumbling wall.

I prefer a gull's scream, empty and clean, when the sea wind reaches into its throat
and a boat pulls away from shore, though what is real is neither purity nor distance

but the place on the wall someone's hand wore away, a cat's eye, a drunk's sleep.
Night sky, voyaging stars, distant space: guide me, instruct me, inhabit my voice.

II

What inn is this where for the night peculiar traveller comes?

—E. Dickinson

PHOTOGRAPH
for Zdena Berger

Here are three children, caught in blurred motion, playing charades on the far side
of a house, where the window is nothing but a wall of white light, flowing as if
from an inexhaustible source.

The glare from the window makes the small bodies
oblique: it looks as if some force were pulling them irresistibly out into the world
on the other side of the glass, where they will go flying far off into blind space,

hurled over seas and continents.

From inside, shadows crowd in on them: the dark wood of a dining table, dusty
plumes by a mirror, a lamp giving thick, circular light, letters propped up against
a vase with purple flowers.

Time-wasted things—a green gingerpot, a bird's nest
found on a walk, a wooden primer with words in a foreign language, lie like objects
in a tomb, accompanying the dead to their next dwelling-place.

On a shelf in a corner, a woman—we share a name—
looks out from the back cover of a book, the air around her face filled with ghosts
from a dark corner of Europe.

Perhaps one night an angel will come and take me
for her, and grant her another life, if only the one meant for a child, a life crying out
from the books she leans against, from gestures of play, from the glowing pane.

17

If

history is the autobiography of a madman
some senior doctor may be well-informed
as to the nature of the patient's delusions,

but we – the next of kin – are quite blind;
we just know if not well watched he may
drink a bottle of bleach "to purify mankind"

but if orderlies wrest the bottle from him
he'll sink into melancholia, markets will
flag, people will start hoarding and no one

will turn up for weekly discussion groups
on electoral reform or atonality in music,
he will grow sluggish, filled with loathing

analysis, if flawed, has been a mainstay
for us in mitigating his worst excesses
in relations with his Lord and Liberté;

at times he seems to grasp that his desire
to possess *her* is fated sadly never to be
wholly satisfied, but he'll never conquer

a fear of being taken from bed at night
and put out *like a dog*; at times
he can name pursuits that give delight:

building with stones of unequal weight,
expeditions into the wilderness, rescue
of beauties, long sums that equal naught

In the North (Westerbork)

Winter came and went, spreading its iron grain;
the earth the color of ash, trees the color of bone.

In an interval between wars, spring and summer
passed, color advertisements for another country.

At a place where trains departed every Tuesday
a stick probes the exhausted mouth of morning;

the North shaves and washes in its cold mirror,
the trees claw at the doors of the earth and air.

The wind throws off its white sheet and wanders,
a wakeful child in a house deserted by the elders.

In icy furrows a thin wind is rubbing its face raw.
On a branch an oriole is punishing its one vowel.

National Resources (Amsterdam)

Stone,
cloud, a stained face,
the bottom of a fountain;

a hard eye, a clear idea,
commerce's flag,
murderous curiosity;

a bitter mouth,
Joseph Roth's mirth,
a barber's cuttings;

a deposit
of raw petroleum,
a tear of Ingrid Jonker.

Windows lit up
with pink neon,
the curtains open.

A trip, a scream,
a leather jacket,
a postcard of death.

Flower vendors,
a man cuts stalks
with thin fingers,

a Turkish girl
jumps off a tram
in high-heeled boots.

Rip a red vein
from the seam
of Rebecca's gown;

fish a needle
from a gutter
or a sluice;

stitch each drop
to the bottom
of the inner eye.

London E5

i

The stone republic raises a chalky face
a snail's tracks mark the cemetery path
and a patriarch's smoke trace disperses

raindrops slouch into a waning garden
it's April's yearly conference of winds
the crows shuffle papers on the Gothic

Time for the rain to burst in and flood
memory's cellar, everything that was
fastened, moored, will drift into view

the steamed-up windows of eel shops
an old conspiracy of scales and beards

ii

Oblivion city,
mongrel tomb,
blinded room,

Fiction's home,
stray dogs, rose leaves:
bed of brick,

rustle of feathers,
drying leaves,
liturgy of smoke

iii

Dreams of sacrifice
still meet to smoke
huddled by the river

Pages you ripped
from a book form
a dam downstream

A brown river
flowing softly
unravels a song

Blake's girl runs
howling down
a highway of flesh

Beaked messengers
appear in dirty elms
along Greek Street:

Are you about
to break the covenant
of dream and will

knit in brass, sealed
with the first frost
of the year's midnight?

Ev'n in their Ashes (Srebrenica-London 1995)

Curfew of summer, the middle nineties,
a labyrinth of blood & plastic, you enter
the elseward crowd in the Underground,

asylum of unkempt children and kidney
merchants & pure products of hysteria
folding maps without an icon for fear,

no one asked for proof of name, *threats
of pain and ruin*, they find each other
without a special Balkan handshake

it doesn't matter where you were born
but how long you've slept on a Morden
train with a blanket torn from *The Sun*;

in the nineties the definition of freedom
is not *kindled at the Muse's flame*, or spun
of dawn love, but a multiple choice form,

a map of the Tube: either an assembly
belt for the City, a flat dead pulse,
or a cage circling, centering, northerly

your journey in steel and hooded glass
through zones of fire, watched by a man
with white eyes right to the edge of town

where you got off & hid in a graveyard,
reading the eighteenth century epitaphs,
picking worms off your legs & thinking

of *pleasing anxious being,* shorn from
eight thousand bodies thrown into a pit
and the bleating of sheep under a knife

KNIFE

From a plush seat in this restaurant
I see it grinning at me like a dandy,
its smooth surface distracting nicely
from the low direction of its thoughts.

As I am talking blandly to my party
it lies between us, a great authority,
an officer in plain clothes, a loose
prosthesis, toy of a tyrannical child.

It has the cunning of a desperado.
Sister, put a chair against the door.
It has the style and charm of a spy.
Waiter, did you see that man arrive?

Hold it not like a gear shift, or a pen.
Hold it so that it doesn't cast a shadow.
Before they carry out a steaming lamb
I've got a taste of metal in my mouth.

WAGNER'S DREAMS
for René Samson

Above the low roofs of the town of Bayreuth,
above its thick air and its slender river,
above the forests of Bavaria, Wagner
is flying. His sideburns flutter. He's asleep,
he's dreaming, Tristan's chord travels
painfully across the German earth.
Wagner's asleep, his strength has ebbed, no more
does he climb trees in the orchards of friends
or slide down their banisters; he's asleep now,
his ego subdued for good. Let him sleep,
let him inhabit his dreams, where he forgets
his years of poverty, his bastard's birth,
his embittered revolutionary pride.
Let him inhabit his dreams, the only place
where he defers to another human being,
shows Dr. Schopenhauer a "flock"
of nightingales the master has already seen;
his dreams, where he defers to compassion,
to the unity of wronged and wrongdoer.
His dreams, where he is finally reconciled
with the phantom otherness of Jews, where
he talks quietly with Mendelssohn,
calling him Du; where his apology
is applauded like a diva's aria.
Let Wagner sleep, let him dwell in his dreams,
don't let him out, let him dream his music,
where he finds belonging beyond blood
and longing tempered by form. Music, where
the sound of redemption is something fresh,
a drink of clear water, a young girl's voice,
a flute. Let him seek refuge in music, where
the sweating bourgeoisie can't flatter him,
where even King Ludwig's search patrol

27

won't track him down. Let him dream,
turn his portrait to the wall, keep the earth
firmly packed on his lips. Let him float
on the wings of music, across a continent
Beethoven explored and left to Mahler,
let him ride "continuous melody" home,
released from the will by grace, a free gift,
or beauty, the same: for the final chord,
resolving our pain, is not written by us.

Two Gods

Two men flew over Hiroshima,
hailed on return by General Spaatz.
Back home, one entered a monastery.
The other embarked on a life of crime
(leaving the money behind on the counter).
His sentence was reduced by the criminal courts
when experts explained his need for punishment.

God of pity, god of wrath

In the South

i

Cicadas:
no history, only
a permanent revolution of seasons.

Rain: an unwanted intimacy of Zeus,
all contact with the crew has been lost.

The city prophet
staggers to a corner store,
crying in tongues that the end of the world is at hand,
followed by a retinue of dogs.

He lies down in the dust, on the asphalt road,
while the cars whip him with shreds of his shirt.

From behind a billboard
promising the salvation of the world
steps the loud constituency of the dead;

a soldier's uniform flies
bodiless over continents,
pockets stuffed with flesh:
a tangle of long grey hair,
pulled from a hairbrush,
still goes hungry.

Dog man,
discover with your cane the edge of the sidewalk,
and cross on the arm of your memory of crossing

ii   Huntsville Prison Museum

Make sure you get an education.
Son, stand at the wooden throne.

Feeble justice, bodyguard death.
Feeble death, plagiarist of justice.

iii   National Orgy

The kick is forcing them to do what they always wanted.
Spell it O-R-G-Y so the kids don't get what you're saying.
An inappropriate joke or remark may lead to your arrest.

iv   Aqui Tambien

Cicadas: a Greek chorus announces
a Gulf storm. Forecasters tremble
with tragic joy. A poet of lost battles
sends his voice into galactic space.
Dogs hear appeals from death row;
cicadas quote the Oresteia in a way
only stones understand or a Mexican
who's ninety years old & not talking;
storms rip down an eight-lane highway
and a cicada arriving in a private jet
left its wings by the side of the pool.

v   (1-800-PINE BOX)

In the mute throat of the country,
lined with dust and plastic, a neon
primer instructs the eye and heart.

Maison des Pestiferez (Flemish print, 17th Century)

Inscribed in two languages,
and circumscribed by water.
Men float on rafts of shadow;
death comes as a liberator.

What do they talk about?
What a glorious morning.
Did you hear that sound?
I had a marvelous dream.

Paris 2001

It was the articulate city's later season,
talk like white noise erasing pain,
streets where Louis Capet still ran,
naked, from the mob. Anger awoke
in the *banlieue*, sweaty diplomats grew lean
keeping Europa above water,
boulevards lay like subjugated armies,
bark peeled from plane trees and the fall
was a judge's reply to a plaintiff's question,
a last word held in common: *September,*

fire, an epidemic of flames broke out
and no firewall was smart enough; on TV
New York policemen spoke perfect French,
but cloud-capp'd towers, gorgeous palaces,
everything was falling, falls repeated
in screens in shop windows. Security checks
at Victoire synagogue, someone shouted
"you deserved it"; God slipped in the back.
We were handed a xerox of Psalm 91—
a parachute, a sheet fastened to the sky.

The Afterlife of Victory
(Pierson Museum of Antiquities, Amsterdam)

Mummies smile: death is the perfect society. Lenin's frown
is the only thing he can display from the other side of glass.

The defeated bring tribute to the new rulers of ancient Iraq.
One carries a model city, one leads a horse too big for him.

Raising the cup, you face Nike pouring a sacrifice to herself.
Why to herself? Is that blood of the last warriors in her cup?

Relics of Cluny

Petrified cross;
a child points:
papa il est laid

indulgences sell;
an image stirs
in a letter's walls

A white hand grows
in a field of rabbits,
Mantegna's garden

But no agony here
No, there's nothing
on sin's menu for her

the weight of a beast's
hoof in her lap
gold standard of virtue

The lion has nothing
to do – she holds
the banner herself

Outside French girls
sit under cumulus
clouds of irony

an old Algerian
polishes a pair
of doll's shoes

an old woman
sits down nearby
asks for a cigarette

she smokes it
holding my hand
fondles the warning

a man in a suit
books a cremation
on a mobile phone

the head waiter
weighs evidence,
sits in judgment

SAN JUAN DEL DUERO

este alma de polvo
de los dias malos
—Machado

Arab coins, an Abrahamic will,
sacred chants a guard switched off
to listen to the latest soccer scores;

when we drove back into the hills
a cloud in the shape of Rodin's Balzac
pursued us and then the storm broke

& the sheep in silent Adealpozo
turned their tails to the rain without
looking up at the sound of the car

Days of 2004

Monday

Cruel, stirring in its cold bed, ice eats the shore with each green wave;
winter is being demolished: next door workmen are stripping a house,
ripping plaster which hits the asphalt with the sound of petrified cloud;
I want to rip winter out of myself, drop it from the window, glass pane,
let trucks take it away – that was your job, that's what you used to do.

Tuesday

The bulbs burned out; the gulls
rise and fall over a bench made
vagabond-proof by four armrests.

Cooing in mid-sleep, a pigeon sits,
a fakir on the lamp's wig of quills.
Choose: pain, flight, sleep or light.

Wednesday (South Side Train, Chicago)

Slowly and with infinite care the trees by the lake are ripping a thousand
plastic bags to shreds

Thursday

A day so hot, insects found the shade of thorns, thorns
the shade of berries, berries that of leaves. The sun,
strangling a linden, got a stranger to take their picture.
A pregnant cat howled like Laocoön in Virgil's poem,
radicalizing the traditional canons of expression, but
the Ministry of Theory had closed for summer recess
and Bohemia's server was down. A scholar took notes,
but the sun conspired with a glass to set them on fire
and all that was left for publication was a heap of ash.

Friday

It was like the day when Ursula set off
for Rome: eleven thousand pure words
embarked with me at dawn. I woke up
in a stranger's house to a smell of mint
and ignored the angel entering the room
like a silent nurse pushing a dinner tray.
A cormorant sat digesting stone. Low
waves lisped, illiterate and worshipful.
Where was I going? Three waters join,
seeking the North. The guidebook's in
another language, I have to carry over
words as heavy and enigmatic as stones
while the river tries to pull them under.

Saturday

Someone must have discovered once it's easier to carry two loads
than one, whether your kids or your food or rocks for a graveyard.
Here is a yoke, chipped at the neck and painted with flowers.

On the façade of the old house, you read *injuria ulciscenda oblivione.*
Two weights hanging on a verb's yoke: to avenge. Until oblivion
balances injury, you can avenge by painting the yoke with flowers.

Sunday

So a street is to be named Milosz?
Sure, and why not, but I reject it.
Not just because it is outrageous
for a man to be laid out in asphalt
or because a monument dissolves
ambivalence, slackening feeling
and I want mine to keep its knots.
Because his path ran by the world's
edges, where in isolation and doubt
he found beauty and knowledge;
because no road on earth shunts
that knowledge back downtown;
poetry hangs out but never dwells.

Vasilevsky Island

In memoriam Galina Starovoitova

The end of a millenial century:
snow laid out the white sheets
to show us how dirty we were.
Death is a cell phone and sweats.

The city lowered its eyelids.
At a bridge, some kids showed us
Bonaparte's face hung between
the hind legs of a horse.

They were making a snowman
and calling it *Great Leader*.
By Christmas it would be dirty;
by New Year, it would be gone.

AKHMATOVA, 1921

The angels had gone crazy, they went on playing
baccarat in their pyjamas until daylight
sent them scurrying off to bed.
Devils lifted dumbbells in the basement.

Our native worlds, our other worlds, untied
from earth's orbit, floated off into other galaxies;
our crimes grew stranger to us than spots on the moon.
In the Tsar's garden, tree trunks were bleeding,

and dawn's spiders were being fitted for uniforms;
people were eating the tender flesh of swallows
and words fled across quickly-changing borders,

but someone had to follow the dead into exile;
someone's face had to grow the right shadows
to make a great spectacle at the whipping post.

Postcards from Kraków

i   **Trakl, Hospital**

Locked ward, padded door,
an arrow points to the exit,
blood on the Empire's cuff;

a wheelchair waits empty,
madness weighs nothing,
the nurse smells of scorn.

Be here near death,
awake to the world,

imperfect reconciliation.

ii   **Hospital, Garden**

A man is burning weeds outside the wards.
Branch and root burn.

On the roof, crows cry.
They may enter the sky without knocking.

iii   **Garden, Calvary**

I hardly speak this language.
Nuns argue with a gardener.

Words fall my side of the wall,
steps lead up to Pilate's palace.

Power is above speech or below it.
He has power who doesn't seek it.

He who sees a wall and behind it
—a garden. I hardly speak this.

iv   **Calvary, Eve**

Snow fell; I smoked and read John.

Why do pain and death make holy?

Out of what 'thou' was death born?

Translation

Patroklos put on the armor
of his good friend Achilles
to go out on the battlefield:

your words, a bright shield
lending cover and honor
will save neither one of us.

Terminal Étude

not on paper but human and bitter —Miron Białoszewski

We're only a little dead:
a shadow broke a window
and found its way to bed
warm enough for a word
narrow enough for a widow
only a fissure in Warsaw

in the middle of Warsaw
who is also a widow
(behind a broken window
she's only a little dead)
I was lying in bed
too tired to read a word

Without a single word
about your being dead
(it's obvious to a widow)
you lay down in bed
and told me about Warsaw
just outside the window

Holding shards of window
you said you had a word
known only to the dead
you whispered it in bed
it sounds a bit like Warsaw
from the mouth of a widow

We made death a widow
more bereft than Warsaw
falling through a window
in the middle of the bed
wrapped in that one word
we raised up the dead

A door leads to the dead
by a fissure in the word
so now all over Warsaw
down to the last widow
we're waiting by a window
till they come back to bed

Now all Warsaw is our bed
and your word is a widow
with a window on the dead

III

among the voices voiceless
that throng my hiddenness

—*S. Beckett*

MATHEMATICIAN

At twenty, I got drunk on Friday nights
at the conservative students' association.
I did analysis on beer mats with a felt pen,
sometimes continuing onto the table.
Once I won a bet with my professor; I
covered two tables and the seat of a chair.
I learned that a voice without undertones
thrown from the back of the mouth draws
a person's attention across several rooms.

At thirty, an associate professor, I lived
with a young girl in a sunny apartment
by a park and spent nights tracing fits
of passion and rage in Beethoven. I tried
to explain to her my notation system
for the *Pathétique*, which put sequences
of notes, trills and dynamic shifts into
equations of exquisite formal elegance.
Last year, no longer a girl, she left.

I lay on the bed not crying or laughing.
I got oranges & let them rot in the nets.
The melody following the tolling bells
in Debussy's *Cathédrale engloutie* is
the most frightening thing I ever heard;
however, the sea rises to drown it out.
I'm now taking singing lessons to learn
to project from the front of the palate.
I want to express every shade of feeling.

I've begun to speak with a softer voice,
gentler, more alone, which is what you've
got to be. I bought a TV and spend nights
watching the war. I want to know how
to find the oasis of strangeness in a desert
of order. I see only the familiar mirages
of certainty, encampments of knowledge.
I'm now working on a symbolic language
which will enable me to elucidate all this.

IMMIGRANT SCHOOL, SAN FRANCISCO

One more time for the camera:
This is an exciting proposition.
As for salary level, I am open.

Your language is a hard one.
But I'm studying every night.
I have an open personality.

My son will become a doctor
like my husband and me. You
see how much it means to us.

Above all I know what I want.
I've studied the tapes closely.
I stand in front of the mirror.

One more time for the camera:
You see how much it means.
You see how much I want.
You see how much I am.

Mondriaan

I note a certain progress in human affairs:
No longer are the signs to be found only
in the privacy of studios and work rooms,
they are writ large on the dancing floors
of Paris and New York! Heels kicking out,
up-and-down movements made by bending
and straightening knees to the syncopated
4-4 rhythm of ragtime jazz: there has been
much to-do about the alleged sinfulness
of the Charleston. My country banned it,
claiming it encourages self-abandonment
and a general decline in moral standards.

I find it, on the contrary, quite sexless.
The couples keep their distance and move
with powerfully maintained concentration
of speed: there's no time for transgression.
I am fond of going to the public dance halls
to hear the taut, strenuous sound of this music,
to see Josephine put us all to shame. I wince
at the cloying plaintiveness of the tango. I like
shapes and sounds to start and stop abruptly.
The futurists are wrong: one must search for
the universal, not the novel; the essential, not
the sensational. They are still too sentimental.

From the Chinese Book of Songs

i

Saved from my own desires, I keep those of others
with me. Guests whose houses burned down have
nowhere to go. It would be cruel to send them off
to visit ruins. There are parts of my mind I haven't
visited for a long time and do not care to visit now.
Let's open this bottle of wine and spit at the moon.

ii

By this liquid window
I can sit in solitude
By this shifting sky
I can sit without intent

Why for a meal of words
must I have a license?
Why for a meal of love
must I have a diploma?

Being of sound mind
I accept a meal of silence
Being of sound body
I accept a meal of pain

iii   **Wild Rain**

Great & violent Heaven. You're witholding something
and meanwhile death rounds up all the usual suspects.
Majesty would seem to consist in having no plan at all.
Violence marries guilty earth with the innocent clouds,
the guilty run smiling toward the marketplace of tears.
Are distant gods subject to karma in decaying heavens?
Our politicians are passing laws to cover their expenses.
Let's open up the files. Let them fall in a plague of frogs.

iv   **Chinese Love Poem**

Dark green trees, a white mist parts:
keep the one you are thinking about
in the air-conditioned part of a mind
flying on its wings of glass and steel
on a long and wearying flight course,
carrying safely what you seek to flee.

Rich green trees, a white mist drifts:
shelve the one whom you don't name
between books in the mind's library
on the *index hominorum prohibitum,*
where if you try to reach him alarms
will go off and guards come running.

Bright green trees, a white mist shines:
see the one for whom there is no sign
just at the edge of vision & turn right,

fall through a window, taste the glass:
behind a screen in the interior of sight
there's no edge, no shelf and no flight.

v   **Thieves' Song**
for Rogi Wieg

What plant is not yellow?
What day is without flight?
What man is not on the go
Thieving in the four cities?

What plant is not black?
What girl not the lookout?
Heigho, for us thieves!
We're not treated as persons.

Neither shrieve nor tease,
Yet we're loose on the streets.
Heigho, for us thieves!
Day and night we don't sleep.

A magpie in a sixpiece suit
Is making a row in the lobby,
While we with a full car boot
Tear along the road of Zhou.

CURRICULUM VITAE

I was born in mid-winter.
A bird obscured the sun.
It was a public holiday:
rubbish stood uncollected
in the streets of the capital.
Soldiers sat smoking
around mountain fires.
My mother wore red,
the doctors wore white,
my father came running.
My education proper
began when my uncle
fell into my room, nude
but for a tumbler of whiskey.
I kissed his knees and feet.
From then on, it was one
mad success after another:
first of my sex allowed to
do rifle training, prizes
in ethnic understanding.
An artist I posed for said
a woman worth painting
looks clumsy in a dress.
At graduation, I recited
and I long and yearn
bringing tears to many eyes.
I believe I am suitable for
the position of his majesty's
concubine for several reasons.
I rarely speak: since I left
school, I've spoken only
to decline marriage offers.

I rarely weep: once, when
my son was taken away.
It's said the emperor likes
games of flight and pursuit.
If I may say so, without
being thought immodest,
I'm an accomplished prey.

NATIVITY

A bird's silhouette on the roof of a shed:
not even a stable, just a stretch of wall
and a narrow shelter where a cow's head
falls down toward a few scattered stalks.

Angels with clean pink mouths gathered
on an icy hillside, the parents practicing
movements of a dumb show. A shepherd
raises his hand as if to start the sacrifice.

God is a child and we are old men; a child
gave birth to us and we have to nurse it;
let the cow give it rich milk, let the bird
feed it hard grains of wheat. Untouched

by our gifts, washed by a beast's tongue,
let it be silent as stone, let it save no one.

LETTER FOUND IN A RUSSIAN NOVEL

My darling Masha,
you told me and I never believed you.

How far away it seemed, like another planet,
cold and foreign.

Both poor, but a match could keep us warm,
strong tea could get us drunk.

Then one of us found the truth –
the path, the way, the faith, etc.
The shrines smelled of resin.

I marched off into the future;
you stood on the threshold not waving but smiling.

Your smile grew inside me like an extra limb,
an organ which God gave to all creatures
but cut out in a fit of jealousy.

I sweated you out of my system
like a fever, an impurity.
I spat you out like a worm
in the apple I was eating.

Pure, I rose to undreamed heights
like a Rococo angel, and looked down on
a world of rosy-cheeked peasants and stately dances.

Pricked, I sailed down to earth
like a red-faced Baron von Münchhausen.
My children have disowned me.

Now only reading
shortens the winter evenings
and I think of you.

Where have you been all these years?
Don't tell me you were recruited
for the legions of the snowy plains.
Don't tell me you fell foul
of our wooden puppeteers.

How could they, verbless, command
a thing or you, my tender word bed,
stubborn bookend, slender fountain pen.

Come back, I implore you;
close your eyes and touch my typewriter keys.
We'll play the Yeatses again,
invoke the Muse in a burst of geriatric strength.

Come back from the icy past, darling,
from the Andante in the 10th Symphony,
into the great and empty air in which we live.

This is a different planet, darling.
Come back to me at once.
I'm frightened without you.

INTERIOR MODEL

Fear love Fear love —*Dora Maar*

I have a yellow chin and one red eye.
The shadow of my lower lip is green.
My other eye looks inward at a greenish
shadow where my faces meet. From two
black sleeves, my yellow fingers grow.
One plucks an ear with a painted nail,
from the left arm, a pale thumb droops.
Peacock plumes fan out from my navel,
tickling my breasts, pointing to my crotch.
He sketches me in haste, with an accent
on my heavy lids and Macedonian nose.

He paints three portraits in a day and then
we fall into bed. When I wake in the dark
he's working again but doesn't let me look.
He watches when I dress my hair and sees
something at once girlish and grotesque.
He hands out reproductions of Guernica
to German soldiers swarming over Paris.
Another night, and my gruesome nudity
sits on the easel, trapped in a dark cell,
with heavy lids and nose. Will he hand out
reproductions of me to his lovers-to-be?

AFTER THE ARABIC
for Najat Goldwasser

1   Abu Nuwas

I write the poetry of the dead
with the hand of one still alive
driven into this corner by fate
I hang between here & beyond
I was left nothing but my body
almost invisible yet still near

You do not recognize me now
not even your eyes could read
these lines printed on my face
I can't be found in any syllable
but an eyelid's flicker is enough
to take this pain from me forever

2   Dialogue of Abu Nuwas and Inan

I have seen the stars shine in morning skies
as if molten gold had been poured over ice.

*I'd make that metaphor with a citric candle
warding flies from an old man's café table.*

3 Ibn 'Iyad

Look: the ripening wheat
bent low by the high winds
like squadrons of soldiers
in flight, bleeding defeat
from the poppies' wounds.

4 Ibn At –Tubi

I am grateful to this sickness unto death;
my fever has granted my petition.

At my side you stand, inaccessible one:
welcome, disastrous short breath.

Pascal, Inventor of the Syringe

What I hate in myself, I destroy in others.
What I don't have I take away from them.
Lord, fill and destroy me with one needle.

POST-HOMAGE

aut illis flamma aut imber subducet honores —*Sextus Propertius*

i

Shades of Tu Fu, Tang landscapes of Po Chü-I,
let me enter into your precincts
I who come from the secular cities
hiding metaphysics in a viola case

How did you learn your stroke,
what academies examined you;
what pain mellowed your tone?

It's reassuring to find that poets laureate
continue to fill the bookstores with verse;
your pebbles cut me when I pick them up
and remind me of the virtues of reticence.

You always traveled lightly but in style;
your summer house is but ten feet square,
yet above the western eaves you often spy
clouds that cap the mountains of T'ai-po.

I admire the "startling new voice"
and the "linguistic tour-de-force"
but how about something to read before an operation?
How about a few lines to engrave on a ring or a stone?
I ask a poem that neither primps nor shirks.

And there's no rush whatsoever;
I've always been a slow worker,
but there are things only I can tell you, late though I am.

Who would know about the wards of Campbell Hospital
or the soldier from Plymouth County, Massachussetts,
a fellow with sensitive and tender feelings,
who was wounded at Fredericksburgh, sent up from the front,
from Falmouth Station,
in an open platform car
(such as hogs are transported upon north)
and dumped with others in Ward 6, *falling down like a rag*
where they deposited him?

No one would know of him, even Lincoln buffs,
if Walt had not passed by that day!

And I among the later daughters of this continent
shall have my work cut out,
and no salary or degree for this ambivalence;
nor, I hope, a lethal contempt.

Book III.1

ii

Interea, a stark regime of arpeggios.

Start with the *Adespota Iambica*, which Plutarch finds
indispensable
to anger management; one may die fulfilled
having scanned
The aged crone called Xanthe, women's friend.

Some say Sappho kept sailors on shore
(with songs?) thus damaging trade;
Archilochos waged love and made war
with equal panache, a poster-boy for hate;

glass sprayed on the balcony, salt in the sheets:
a storm that wound the spring of lust and jealousy
for three millenia had come across the sea.

Every chip of his memorial on Paros
also bears witness to his crimes—
each seed spilled will have a separate courthouse
and a separate trial.

Happy those who appear in his footnotes,
his book will be a pillow for their heads.
But apart from that?

Neither the cut grass at Forest Lawn,
nor all the war memorials in Europe,
nor all the proposals for Ground Zero
add a thing to our knowledge of death.

Fire frays, rain seeps, the years' heels beat all into the ground.
Ruins are what we have instead of Nature.
But the clear light of the mind knows no hours or years,
and some names remain untouched by death.

Book III .2

iii

I saw you in a dream, *mea vita*, stranded,
waving powerless to passing traffic
amid headlights ploughing darkness,
in your mouth all quarrels were ended
but you couldn't see me,
your fedora sagging under torrents of rain
like the hero of a reel of damaged film
whose pick-up never comes
and he disappears into a river of light.

I was seized by fright,
saw the road grow a shrine and flowers,
strangers slowing down to look, quake,
then step on the gas and speed away.

I called Apollo by every name,
muse and medic, and Hermes too, of roadside luck,
and offered them what I had fit, gifts of guilt and id.

Then you were sinking down in the gutter
and I had to go on watching
deafened by swelling music, when you fell.

You rolled back into the margins of a plot
so tangled no one would find a trace of you
or tell you whose side you were on,
or where you could find your car.

A pale woman appeared beside you
and slung your arm over her bare shoulder.

And I was running to you across the highway
when I awoke, gasping, on the bedroom floor.

Book II.26

iv

Let others speak of you, or be without a name,
a man who sows in barren earth will praise you.
One day your gifts will all go down in the grave
and the place will harvest nothing but contempt,
not even a spat-out: "The ashes of a learned girl."

Book II.11

V

You mortals, then,

befriend the uncertain hour of death,
discover what road will lead it to you:
scour the skies like an old Phoenician
for the stars of luck and stars of none.

Whether you pick them off by day
or move in squads of golden youth
by night, the perils of earth and sky
are encrypted in an unbroken code.

You cry that the "win" eludes you
now Mars joins ranks on either side,
and in the burning house, the ruins,
no cup left to drink even darkness.

Only a lover knows when he'll end
and in what fashion; he won't fear
storms, quakes or kangaroo courts,
nor even weapons of mass deception.

If he be halfway across the Styx,
well within sight of the infernal prow,
his lover need but whisper—he'll
return by the path of no known law.

Book II: 27

vi

When, only when and when without fail death sends its representative,
fast falling naked through the mind's surface
and away from all those, bosses and partners,
to whom we thought we were eternally bound, one tangle of darkness.

The President will go on plotting against Evil,
Tigris and Euphrates flow at his command,
the territories will swarm with special forces,

the heathens will adopt our uniforms and pay tribute to our gods,
to whom we thought we were eternally bound, one tangle of darkness.

My funeral will not be a fancy occasion, with me no dynasty will end;
        My death will leave no great hole in the fabric of being;
it won't take place in a Paris hotel; the press will have nothing on file.
A simple affair.
        Enough, more than enough to go there
clutching a few books on my bed of flowers
        to provide Persephone with identification.

You will follow stripped and frightened thoughts
& call my name deep in the night, if it is allowed
        you'll kiss my face
        your pound of flesh
        with its doors shut

        "She who is an empty cage
        housed a flock of wild birds"
That much I would like on my stone
        "Death, I don't have all day."

You will feel some pain at the absence,
    that seems to be part of a deal,
we miss those we love & who miss us,

even when they die without a show, off camera,
without appointing any successors or executors.
    It's no use calling on the dead, it's pure vanity.
Vanity to make such demands of your own dead.
    And anyway, my bones' small talk would bore you.

Book II: 13A

Notes

"Orphan Fire xii": The italicized phrase is translated from Paul Celan, "Unter ein Bild" (Under a Painting), from the collection *Sprachgitter* (1959).

"Orphan Fire xix": The italicized phrase is David Grene's translation of the opening phrase of Herodotus' *Histories*, Book 2.99.

"Orphan Fire xvii: Fear": The italicized phrase is translated from Ludwig Wittgenstein's diaries of 1930-32 and 1936-1937, published as *Denkbewegungen* (1997).

"If": The first line is quoted from the Russian author Alexander Herzen.

"Ev'n in their Ashes (Srebrenica-London 1995)": italicized quotations are from Thomas Gray, "Elegy Written in a Country Graveyard."

"In the South" section 3: the italicized phrase was broadcast repeatedly on the intercom system at George W. Bush International Airport in Houston, Texas, in the months after September 11, 2001.

"Days of 2004: Saturday": the Latin phrase translates as: "oblivion will avenge injury."

"Vasilevsky Island": Galina Starovoitova was a Russian democratic politician, assassinated in St. Petersburg in November 1998.

"Postcards from Kraków": the Austrian poet Georg Trakl died, presumably a suicide, in a psychiatric ward in Kraków, Poland, in 1915.

"Terminal Étude": the title refers to one of the terminals at Frederic Chopin International Airport in Warsaw, Poland. The epigraph is from M. Białoszewski's poem "Sen" (Dream).

"Post-Homage": Book numbers refer to Sextus Propertius' elegies, with which these poems take liberties; sections I and VI also refer to Ezra Pound's free versions of those elegies in "Homage to Sextus Propertius."

ACKNOWLEDGMENTS:

Grateful acknowledgment is made to the journals in which some of these poems first appeared:

The Antioch Review, Free Lunch, Magma, The North, Pleiades, Ploughshares, Poetry ("In the North," "Mathematician," "Orphan Fire vi: Atomic Love Poem," and "Orphan Fire vii: Body"), *TriQuarterly, Women's Review of Books,* and *Verse.*

"Wagner's Dreams" is a collaboration with the composer René Samson, whose piece for baritone and piano quartet under the same title was first performed in September 2007 as a part of the Festival Haaglanden, in the Glazen Zaal in The Hague.

I owe warm thanks to James Kastely, Rich Levy, Inprint, Inc., and Lillie Robertson of Houston, Texas, for generous fellowship (and moral) support during work on this book; to the Illinois Arts Council, Ruth Lilly and Joseph Parisi of Chicago for similar support; to Anne Carson, Harry Clifton, Mark Doty, Louise Glück, Philip Levine, Robert Mezey, Miho Nonaka, and C.K. Williams for merciless encouragement at various stages, and, above all, to Edward Hirsch and Adam Zagajewski for vital doses of warmth and lucidity. For the existence of this book I'm hopelessly indebted to the incomparable Ilya Kaminsky.

I am deeply grateful to Sally Ball, Lytton Smith and the whole splendid crew at Four Way Books for their painstaking and passionate work; to Brian Barker, Nicky Beer, Jeff Bernard, Jacob Blakesley, Aaron Crippen, Kathy Garlick, Landon Godfrey, Jennifer Grotz, Eric Gudas, Gary Hawkins, Marc McKee, Katia Mitova, Benjamin Paloff, Todd Samuelson, Sandra Tarlin, and Andrew Zawacki for brazen acts of poetry and friendship; I will always be in loving debt to Ria Loohuizen, to James and Gabriel Leigh-Valles, to Lise and Misha—and, of course, to Leonard: old stanchers and new blessings.

Alissa Valles was born in Amsterdam to an American father and a Dutch mother. She grew up in the United States and the Netherlands and studied Slavic languages, literature and history at the School of Slavonic & East European Studies in London and later at universities in Poland, Russia, and the United States. She has worked for the BBC, the Dutch Institute of War Documentation, the Jewish Historical Insitute and La Strada International in Warsaw, and now works as an independent writer, editor and translator in the Bay Area. She has contributed to *Polish Writers on Writing* (Trinity University Press, 2007), *The New European Poets* (Graywolf, 2008), *Documentary Theatre on the World Stage* (Palgrave Macmillan, 2008) and served as editor for the web journal *Words Without Borders*. Her poems and translations have appeared in *The Iowa Review, The New Yorker, The New York Review of Books, Ploughshares, TriQuarterly, Verse*, the anthology *Strange Attractors: Poems of Love and Mathematics* (A.K. Peters Ltd, 2008), and elsewhere. She is the editor and co-translator of Zbigniew Herbert's *The Collected Poems 1956-1998* (Ecco), a *New York Times Book Review* Notable Book of the Year in 2007, and of Herbert's *Collected Prose*, forthcoming from Ecco in 2009.